# Pricing Strategy

## How to price a product

Bill McFarlane

# Income Disclaimer

This book contains business strategies, marketing methods and other business advice that, regardless of my own results and experience, may not produce the same results (or any results) for you. I make absolutely no guarantee, expressed or implied, that by following the advice below you will make any money or improve current profits, as there are several factors and variables that come into play regarding any given business.

Primarily, results will depend on the nature of the product or business model, the conditions of the marketplace, the experience of the individual, and situations and elements that are beyond your control.

As with any business endeavor, you assume all risk related to investment and money based on your own discretion and at your own potential expense.

# Liability Disclaimer

By reading this book, you assume all risks associated with using the advice given below, with a full understanding that you, solely, are responsible for anything that may occur as a result of putting this information into action in any way, and regardless of your interpretation of the advice.

You further agree that our company cannot be held responsible in any way for the success or failure of your business as a result of the information presented in this book. It is your responsibility to conduct your own due diligence regarding the safe and successful operation of your business if you intend to apply any of our information in any way to your business operations.

# Terms of Use

You are given a non-transferable, "personal use" license to this book. You cannot distribute it or share it with other individuals.

Also, there are no resale rights or private label rights granted when purchasing this book. In other words, it's for your own personal use only.

# Pricing Strategy

## How to price a product

# Table of Contents

# 1. First Things First...

This book has been written primarily aimed at selling
something online but pretty well all of the principles
discussed can be used offline as well. I mention this now
to avoid having to say something every time the word
"online" or similar is used. So, without further ado...

# 2. Let's Get Started!

Have you ever been asked by a potential customer how much something you haven't priced up yet costs for them to buy? Stumped for an on the spot answer to that question? That situation happens more often than you might think and it leaves most people with a fierce internal battle raging in their head. You don't want to under price and make less than you could have but you also don't want to over price and put people off buying.

Let me ask you another question. The last time you launched your own product to sell online, or even offline, how did you come to a conclusion about what price you were going to be selling at?

At a guess, I'd probably say you looked at the competition to see what they were charging. While this is a good start, it's far from the whole picture, and you're fumbling in the dark if looking at the competition is the only factor you're taking into account.

Did you know you can double your sales volume by doubling your price? I've done it myself, and I'll show you how.

Did you also know that 99% of the products I see being sold are too cheap. So much so, that they're actually putting customers off instead of attracting them!

Let's dispel some pricing myths and dig right down to the real facts to ensure you get the most cash in your pocket the next time you launch one of your products.

# 3. Broad Overview

This book aims to cover the following in sufficient detail to get you going with your pricing needs whatever your business or service.

- Introduce the concepts of fluid pricing strategies, and to show that you have many more avenues to explore than it seems like at first glance.

- Answer some of your questions about how you should price your product for maximum profit taking the number of sales to price ratio's into account.

- Illustrate the effect of pricing too low, where many people price their products without first looking at the all important bigger picture.

- Show you why many people are under pricing their products in a big way, and how you can avoid this pitfall.

- Show you that the price you choose for your product isn't simply about charging less than the competition, in fact by charging more, you can be making even more sales.

- Give you additional pricing options for your main product, and show you how you can significantly increase your profits simply through giving your customers options.

- Demonstrate the correct and most effective way of going about introducing trial periods for your products, and why many get this wrong.

- Show you effective methods of experimenting with your price over time without annoying the people who bought from you previously at a higher price.

# 4. Strategies For Pricing Your Products/Services

I know it's temping to jump right in and start slapping prices on products so they can be put up for sale but before you rush off and create a sales funnel, or system, build and upload a website and stick prices on your products there are a few things we need to talk about first.

The goal of this book is to give you some insight into the versatility you have as a marketer with your own products. The problem is, most people just seem to whack a price on their products with little time spent thinking about it. Why they've priced it like that and what factors are going to contribute to whether it's a successful decision. Sound complicated and a lot of work? Well, let me tell you it's not.

But I believe it's really important that I show you just how much freedom to experiment you have with regards to pricing and what effect getting it wrong can have in a number of ways. So before you put a price on your product and release it to the world, take some time out, have a read, pick up the points and take them into account using them as kind of a checklist.

## 4.1. The Wider View

There is a much larger picture to this than the majority of people realize. Often prices are thrown on, just because they can be and possibly fitted loosely around competition and other products and services offering similar things, however, it's not just about a number and planting a dollar sign behind it. All through this process you should be asking yourself lots of why questions. Some of the time, people ask me why the heck I go so in depth into subjects and talk about why they happen. They just want to know how to make a whole load of cash real quick.

Well, I say to them I can tell you a price for a product, but if the situation changes, and you didn't know why that price was recommended in the first place, then you're going to have to come right back to me again, hand me another five hundred dollars just to find out a new price for the same thing in different circumstances. However, if I tell you how things work, you can take some serious knowledge and know-how away with you, and you have the power to adapt to the fast paced changing world of business online or indeed offline. If you can't adapt, you're dead. Or your business is anyway.

Like I say, there's quite a lot to this, and a lot of things that we're going to talk about, and there's going to be a load of questions that are going to pop into your head:

- Does competition matter in such a big marketplace with regards to pricing?

- Should I be cheaper?

- Should I be more expensive?

- How do I know when to be which and why?

- Should I give special offers to particular groups of people?

  - Who?

  - Why?

- Should I offer different versions of my product at different prices?

- How do I do that, and how do I know if I'm doing it right?

There's a load of answers about the above and much more that I'm going to give you in a moment. But all the way through this I want you to keep in mind the flexibility you have as an online marketer with your pricing. Get this right, and it could easily mean double the profits for you. Get it wrong, and it's likely you'll have trouble selling anything at all.

## 4.3. The Competition Pricing Trap

There are a number of pitfalls which I really want you to avoid. I'll try and address them all throughout this book.

What I like to call "the competition pricing trap" is the first of these and we'll address that in this section.

With the formalities and generalizations out of the way, lets get stuck into the meat of pricing strategy and take a look at how you should price your products with regard to competition. The reason I want to talk about this first is simple. When you're looking at pricing, the very first thing you're likely to do is say, "Hey, so what is everyone else charging for similar products?" and picking a price just under your competition.

Now there's nothing wrong with looking at your competition's pricing as a starting point, but there's more to think about, and a number more questions to ask than a simple "can I beat what this guy is charging for his service?"

Your price doesn't have to beat everyone else's out there for you to get sales. This is something that I learned a long time ago, and you may remember me talking about actually increasing my sales by putting the price of the monthly membership up, and offering an option that was actually ten times more money up front, which increased profits even further.

A big take away for you here is that "turnover is vanity, profit is sanity". What that means is that you shouldn't focus on making more sales - increasing turnover - but you should be concentrating on increasing your profit. You may be able to do this by selling less product for a higher price. There is a balance to be struck and that can only be found by testing price points (more on this later).

You really need to be aware of what other people are charging for their products, but that doesn't by any means signal that you have to go out there and undercut them.

Imagine you've just started up an ad tracking and autoresponder script site that's so detailed, and so professional that it smacks the pants off the competition. But you see the other sites offering the same service are hanging around at the ten dollar per month mark. Does this mean that you have to go and beat them and have a lower price before anyone will look at you? Nope, not at all. What you have on your hands is a premium product, and you shouldn't be worried to sell it at a premium price.

## 4.4. Superior Products Sell At Superior Prices

I'm going to give you some of my personal "rules" in this book to help guide you through the pricing minefield. Hopefully they will give you an initial framework to work in to avoid the main roadblocks and set you on the right track.

So, here's rule number one. If you have a great premium product, don't be afraid to bump the price up. You do not by any means have to beat the price of the competition to be competitive. In fact, by putting your price up, it's quite possible that you'll outsell your cheaper competition.

Why? Because a higher price screams quality. Don't, for one moment, believe you have to have the lowest price to make sales. That is simply not true. You just have to have the best sales system, and of course a premium product if you want anyone to actually buy from you again.

## 4.5. Attention Grabbing With Low Prices Spells Doom!

Following on from what we've just discussed, if you're attempting to grab attention by pricing your quality product or service at a ridiculously low price what is most likely going to happen is your customers will look at that and be wondering why the heck you're charging that tiny amount.

If your brand spanking new piece of advanced technology software, for example, is really as good as you say it is, why does it only cost ten dollars?

So here we have rule number two: Never price yourself so low that potential customers think "wow, look at how little that costs. There can't be much to it.". You may think people will look and think "wow that's a quality sounding product, look how little it costs, it's a fantastic deal" but I'm afraid that's not usually what they're saying at all. They're far more likely to be saying the first quote above.

So in effect, all you're doing here is adding even more perceived value to your product through a higher price. It might be the same product, but I tell you now, it's much more likely to sell more copies at a price that someone might look at and think that it's reasonable, or average than something someone might look at and fall off their chair at how cheap you are. It's all about perceived value.

## 4.6. Scared?

Rule Three: Don't be frightened to value your product properly, charge what it's worth.

What I mean by that is so many people are afraid to take the leap and price their products as they believe they're worth. Too many people look at competition and think they have to cost less otherwise no one is going to buy their stuff, or they'll make less money out of it. This is simply not true. Don't undervalue yourself just for the sake of being cheaper. If you have a better product, you put a higher price tag on it. The experimentation and playing around to find the right combination of offers, deals, follow-up and pricing options can come later.

I could show you so many products that are out there right now, in competition with each other, but one is charging a heck of a lot more than the other. Just think about cars for a moment. There are some very successful brands of car out there that charge many times as much as other brands but they are still profitable companies.

## 4.7. Don't Be A Bargain Basement Dinosaur

It's a common urge to create a cheap product and sell it for a chap price but that may not be the best way to go. The thinking is that people always want to pay as little as possible for everything they buy but that really isn't the case. Some things quality isn't an issue and you want the cheapest but most often the price of a product isn't the only or even the overriding factor. Think about the latest purchase you made for your house, whether it was a whole kitchen refit, a new garage door, a toaster, a dinner table, or something else, whatever it was. I bet if you think about it, you'll see that times have changed.

A long time ago, even before I was born, people wanted things that worked. They were functional but just ok. Ok looking and performed the task to a satisfactory degree. But nowadays that's not enough. It's got to be the best, the fastest, the nicest, the easiest to use. There's a real market for premium products emerging. Make sure you don't place yours in the bargain bin if it's meant as premium product, not a bargain basement product.

Need proof? Just look at the automotive industry. People will pay hundreds of thousands for an exclusive supercar which at the end of the day performs exactly the same function as a standard compact - getting you from A to B. There most definitely is room in the car market for premium products, just as there is in your market.

## 4.8 Pick A Card, Any Card - The Magic Of Choice

Next is rule four: Offer pricing options for everything possible. You may be surprised at the range of options for doing this open to you. Think a little beyond the obvious and you'll probably come up with a whole raft of alternative pricing options you can trial with your customers.

Enough about the actual value of your product or service and charging the right amount for it. I want to talk about something else that's rarely done, especially in the world of online marketing and info products. That is offering different price plans from the word go. Sure people might change their price, put it up and down to experiment, put on offers and so on, but that's not doing much if your original plan isn't well thought out.

Even with the simplest of single sale info products such as this, you're presented with options. The more, the better to be honest. Whether you're a high ticket item offering smaller chunks to be paid at extended periods, or a low priced membership site that does the opposite, and offers a lump sum that gives access for three months, six months or even a year.

Another way of offering pricing options is to offer product options as well. What I mean by product options is offering a cut down, or "lite", version for a lower price if that's possible with your product. Or you could look at it from the other end of things and add charged for extras (note these are different from bonuses which we'll talk about later) to increase perceived value and charge more for it.

Remember, the sales process is all about answering the customer's questions, and squashing their fears or any problems they may come up with in their minds for not buying your product. It's no good you selling someone on something and then they find out they don't have the payment option they want. Make sure you add multiples of these. It's simple, if there's anyone out there with a website that only offers one payment option, they're losing sales. Don't let this be you.

## 4.9. A Mutually Rewarding Experience

Rule five, and one of the most important. Never ever, no matter what you do, ignore the people that have purchased from you before. It's not hard to come up with ways to reward them. Right now, I'm putting together an ID number system for myself that allows previous customers to come along and buy my stuff at a discounted rate.

These people are the most important of all. You've already got them on your lists, they've already bought your stuff, which means they're willing to spend money, and of course they trust you, and they're serious about wanting more information, or the products and services you offer. Remember this, because if you forget you'll go broke. It's as simple as that. You want to keep the customers that are buying from you happy, and you want to stay in touch with them. If you don't go out of your way to please them, you'll have to go out and spend wads more on finding new customers. Look after them, because they'll be with you for a long time to come and will form the base of a successful business from the word go.

## 4.10. Tire Kickers

It may be a cliche when some one comes to view a car for sale that they'll walk round it and kick the tires in an attempt to look like they know what to look out for and how to test a car but really they just came to be nosy, they had no real intention of buying the car. Well it's the same story online. There are no tires to kick but the same types of people exist everywhere. They're interested because it's free, not because they're actually interested in the product or service.

Rule number six: Avoid free trials unless you're aiming for lead generation. The problem with free trials is that you'll attract all sorts of freebie seekers and tire kickers. Just like I don't want anyone here that doesn't want to make a successful business of themselves, I'm sure you don't want people wasting your time either, taking up valuable resources and just picking something up because it's free.

As I learned with my big experiment site back in the day, it's far better to charge a small amount for a short trial, say one to three dollars for the first week simply to sort those people out that are coming to you just because they can, and those that are coming to you because they're serious.

I've got a great example for you here too. Now a good friend of mine set up a site when we were in our early days on the scene. He had a pretty good product backed up by a multi level affiliate system, or a matrix of sorts. Anyway, he started promoting and all was going well, until word started spreading around some of his affiliates about some guaranteed signups site that sold signups to anything free, for a fee.

Now unfortunately I'm sure you can see what's coming.

Not only did the affiliates go for this one, which wasn't much help to them, because of course most of these untargeted people were just freebie seekers signing up because they were getting something in return from the guaranteed signups sites, and only a tiny percentage were actually going for his hosting package or the pay plan he had in place. What he ended up with was a system clogged full of people that had no idea what they were subscribing to, weren't making him or themselves or the people that referred them any money, and had no interest in doing so. A real resource disaster case, that one, because it rendered the pay plan almost useless. Make sure you do this one right and offer a trial for a small fee if your product permits. You could be looking at a similar costly situation otherwise.

## 4.11. A Word You Should Never Use

I'm going to reveal a word to you that you may well be using in your business at this very moment which could be costing you untold numbers of sales. It's a word you never want to be associated with your goods and services by the buying public.

Rule seven: Never tell anyone your product is cheap. Yuck. Nothing major to dwell on here, really, but never ever describe your products as cheap. Competitively priced - yes, the best price for that service - yes, cheap - no way. That just devalues your product full stop. You've heard the phrase "cheap and nasty" before right? More often than not, people don't want cheap. They want quality at a good price - value-, especially in online business.

## 4.12. Experimentation

With all the experience in the world and all the knowledge in the world you can never know 100% for sure if a particular price point will work or not with your target market until you actually test it. Testing is vitally important and is one of the most forgotten about things to do in business.

Rule eight: Don't be afraid to experiment with pricing strategies. I can understand how you might be worried that customers, who bought your product costing four hundred dollars, would be annoyed that they receive an e-mail for a special seasonal offer cutting that cost in half, but it seriously doesn't work that way. You're not offending anyone by doing this, and it's the only way you'll come up with new techniques and tactics yourself, through testing.

The fact is real world businesses do this all the time. They have super sales, then they put prices up at Christmas time and particular times of the year when their products are going to be more in demand, discount things daily, add and remove discounts and so on. It's not a wrong thing to do. It's not unethical. It's business. And if your customers have ever left their houses to go and purchase something from a store, they'll know this too.

So here's the deal. If you need some extra cash, why not offer a limited number of members, a long subscription at a discount of a month or so throughout the year? I have to say this one works real well, and I had a large percentage of my member base from my previous site hand me large up front wads of cash that I could put to good use making more cash. If I'd left them at their twenty dollar per month fee, I might have made an extra few hundred dollars, but at a slower pace.

There's nothing wrong with you adding discounts to the end of five or six day follow-up messages, so on and so forth. In fact, there's nothing wrong with changing your price on your main page without any warning or notice. Don't fall into the trap of worrying what previous customers are going to say, because seriously, this happens in the real world all the time. I know in all my experimental days I've never had someone come to me and shout or complain because I pulled a quarter off the price a day after they bought it. If you have a quality product, that's good enough, not to mention you owe it to yourself to try different methods like in the above examples until you get things absolutely perfect.

## 4.13. Adding Value

The best way of adding perceived value is to add genuine value. It is easier to hype things up and create falsely perceived value and that may gain you a quick profit in the very short term but it will lead to long term problems. Your customers will want refunds and never buy from you again, those that don't ask for refunds will simply never buy from you again and they will all tell every one they know not to do business with you. At worst you could end up in jail for fraud so really, don't do it! Adding real value takes a bit more time and effort but the rewards are immeasurably greater and they will likely be long lasting.

Rule nine: Always add value. We've got a whole section that talks about adding value in a moment, through bonuses, different approaches, promo's, and the like. But for now, remember when coming up with a price for your product, don't let it be the only product. Strange sentence indeed, but look at it this way, what kind of things are going to allow you to increase your price and actually persuade people to buy your stuff at the same time?

The quality of your product and sales system are the obvious, but how about bonuses? What about testimonials from known and trusted people in your field? It's not just material things either. What about your reputation and how others see you? So here's a final tidbit of advice for you. If you feel that your product isn't worth the four hundred dollars you're charging then increase its value through these methods. If you still don't feel it's worth it, then at this point, you know that you're charging too much for it.

Ok, I'll be honest with you. If you want to succeed and get your price just right, without being 'cheap' you have to do a little work. A little research and a little brain work. It's not all straight forward one two three. Understand that it's not about being cheaper than anyone else, it's about pricing your product correctly depending on competition, who you're aiming your product at, its quality, and your research and tracking results.

By now you should have a clear idea how much you want to charge, and how you're going to go about it. If you have, great. Just remember, the price you put up there on launch day doesn't have to be set in stone by any means. It's there to be tinkered and played with by you until you feel it's correct, and your testing shows you that it's correct. Have a little confidence in your stuff. Next time you create that amazing info product, membership site, or piece of software, try to avoid selling it at rock bottom prices, because I assure you, it's not gaining you sales, it's losing you them.

## 4.14. Rules Round Up

Rule one: Don't price your product or service too low, charge what it's really worth.

A low price doesn't necessarily mean more profit. You may or may not sell fewer with a higher price but your low price may be so low that you can't sell enough to make up the difference. A higher price can be far more profitable than a lower price and it is profit that is important.

When you're looking at pricing, the first thing that would probably spring to mind if I sent you off right now to price up your products is "what is the competition charging? I'm going to charge less."

Keep in mind from the start, your price doesn't have to match or beat everyone else's, or even come close to doing so for your products to be a success.

You do need to be aware of what others are charging for similar products, but that doesn't mean you need to beat them. Why can't your product be the Mercedes or the Aston Martin of your chosen market? It's still a car, but it's the best, a premium product and the price reflects that.

So, rule number one - If you have a great premium product, don't be afraid to bump the price up - leads nicely into...

Rule two: Price can reinforce perceived value. A higher price can often make your product or service appear more valuable than the competition, but don't price higher than what your product is actually worth until you have a brand position that can command a further premium.

By putting your price up and above the competition, you're actually likely to outsell super cheap competition. Why? Simple. Would you expect the same quality from a

$10 course as from a $1000 one? So there we have rule number two. Never price yourself so low that people think "that product must be really cheap and nasty at that price" even if you think they'll be saying "wow what an amazing deal". You might know your product is of the highest quality but some one who's never bought from you before doesn't and they will take your price into account when deciding what value to attach to your product.

In effect, all you're doing here is adding even more value to your product through a higher price. It might be the same product, but I'll tell you now, it's much more likely to sell at a price someone will think is reasonable, than something that knocks the reader off their chair at how cheap it is.

Rule three: Don't join the crowds who are too afraid to even attempt to bump their prices up. Don't undervalue your product for the sake of being cheaper.

If you have a better product, you go ahead and put a higher price on it. People will soon hear about how you're worth every penny.

I could show you so many products that are out there right now, in competition with each other, but one is charging a heck of a lot more than the other.


Rule four: Offer as many price choices to your customers as possible.

A Pro and a Lite version for example. Not everyone can afford a premium product, and a lite version is just the ticket.

Selling premium products is all well and good (and it is good), but when the price starts to get a little higher, you need to cater to those who can't buy in one go as they may do with less expensive products. An installment plan is a good option in these cases.

Rule five: Reward schemes. It's not hard to come up with ways to reward existing customers. You might like to allow previous customers to come along and buy your stuff at a discounted rate.

You may have seen news reports from around the world about customers of utilities, insurance companies and banks complaining bitterly that the great offers they see advertised on TV by companies they already use are for new customers only. As a loyal existing customer they get nothing and it bugs people.

Existing customers are often the most important of all. You've already got them on your lists, they've already bought your stuff, which means they're willing to spend money, and of course they trust you, and they're serious about wanting more information, or the products and services you offer.

Remember this, because if you forget you'll go broke. It's as simple as that. You want to keep the customers that are buying from you happy, and you want to stay in touch with them. If you don't go out of your way to please them, you'll have to go out and spend wads more on getting new customers. Look after them, because they'll be with you for a long time to come and will form the base of a successful business from the word go.

Rule six: Avoid free trials.

Trial periods are often a standard feature for software or a membership site, but unless you want to waste your time and resources on freebie seekers. Instead set up a low cost, limited trial for them. A dollar for the first month for example, otherwise you might find yourself wondering why your customers aren't buying anything more from you. It's likely because they didn't want to buy in the first place, a waste of your time.

Paying a token amount will get rid of the tire kickers to a great extent and also getting some one to pay you something, even just one solitary dollar starts building trust and also plants a seed of giving you money in their subconscious mind. This can be a very powerful tactic.

Also charging a token amount for a trial will help to prevent unscrupulous affiliates generating useless paid for signups that never buy anything. They never had any intention of buying anything in the first place, they only signed up because they were paid to.

Rule seven: Never say your product is cheap.

It's cost effective, a good deal, good value, but never cheap, which suggests a lack of quality. Remember the old phrase "cheap and nasty".

Rule eight. Test and experiment with pricing strategies.

You can't know what the "sweet spot" is for the price of a particular product, high enough to get the maximum it's worth without pricing it out of the market. Low enough to be affordable and to be seen as worth the money but not so cheap you're doing your self out of profits.

Some people in business are frightened that a customer who paid a higher price one day will see a lower price the next day and be angry with you. This really doesn't happen Walk around your town center or local mall and you'll see sale signs up all over the place. Price changes are happening all the time, people know it's a normal thing to happen.

Also clever use of pricing strategy can come to your aid if you need some extra cash in a hurry. Run a limited time offer or the next x number of people to buy a membership get a long subscription at a discount of a month or so throughout the year? This one often works realy well. One time I did it I had a large percentage of my member base from my previous site hand me large up front wads of cash that I could put to good use elsewhere making more cash. If I'd left them at their twenty dollar per month fee, I might have made an extra few hundred dollars, but at a slower pace and wouldn't have been able to invest in the new profit generating venture.

Rule nine. Always add value.

The next chapter addresses the area of bonuses and other value increasing methods. But for now, remember when coming up with a price for your product, don't let your product be the only product. What kind of things are going to allow you to increase your price and actually persuade people to buy your stuff? In other words what additional things can you add to your product to increase it's value?

The quality of your product and sales system are the obvious, but how about bonuses? What about testimonials from known and trusted people in your field? It's not just material things either. What about your reputation and how others perceive you? Your brand. Building a strong brand can make a huge difference to your bottom line over a period of time. That is a long term strategy but it can be an exceptionally profitable one.

So here's a final tidbit of advice for you in this section. If you feel that your product isn't worth the four hundred dollars you're charging then increase its value through these methods. If you still don't feel it's worth it, then at this point, you know that you're charging too much for it, and your tracking data will also tell you this.

## 4.15. Further Thoughts

I'll be honest with you. If you want to succeed and get your price just right, without being 'cheap' you have to do some work, some research and a bit of brain work. It's not all straight forward A, B, C. Understand that it's not about being cheaper than anyone else, it's about pricing your product correctly depending on competition and relative quality/value, who you're aiming your product at, its quality, and your ongoing tracking and testing.

You will probably have a reasonably clear idea of how much you want to charge for your goods and services using the nine rules above. Remember that the price you put up there on launch day isn't set in stone by any means. It's there to be tinkered and played with by you until you feel it's correct. Have confidence in your products. Next time you create that amazing info product, membership site, or piece of software, try to avoid selling it at rock bottom prices, because I assure you, it's not gaining you sales, it's losing you them!

# 5. Introducing Increased Value

It may sound all well and good to just "increase the value" of a product but how? You can add value before or after the sale of your products or better still, both. This will keep your customers happy, and ultimately be putting more money in your pocket.

Added value can come in many forms, we'll go over some of the best ones in this chapter. This chapter will show you how to:

- Start looking around you, and to start seeing what other people are doing with their value adding, especially the successful ones.

- Take your testimonials further to inspire solid confidence in you and your company from the customers perspective.

- Look closely at standard bonuses, and to avoid some of the pitfalls of other marketers not in the know, who destroy their sales by trying to add value incorrectly.

- Give you three real life examples of real marketers that have tried to add value, but done so incorrectly in one way or another, and to show you how to avoid devastating your sales by doing the same.

- Show that rewarding loyalty goes a long way to increasing sales, and sometimes producing multiple sales from a single product, that means multiplying the profit in your pocket.

31

- Demonstrate how a simple technique will make sure that your customers remember you and your product for a long time to come, leading to further sales down the line, and nice bulge in your pocket.

## 5.2. So How Do We Do it?

The question of how to add value is often seen by business people as being very difficult but it needn't be. This section aims to address those fears and outline real, practical, strategies you can implement in your business while avoiding the mistakes many marketers make.

How to directly influence your sales through the addition of value for your products, ranging from offers, joint venture deals, consultation fees, bonuses and others. You see, it's all about perceived value, and getting the most out of your product.

Again, something we talked about in an earlier section, was getting the price you think your product deserves and persuading people to buy it by stacking on reasons for them to do so, something once mastered, will push people over the edge again and again, buying your products like they're going out of fashion.

There are many ways of pulling this off, and they're forever changing. Marketers are coming up with more and more innovative ways to add value to their products. It's worth watching, in fact, next time you find yourself reading through a sales letter or some ad copy, look at how they add value to their offer using things that aren't directly related to the product itself. Watching how others do things on their sites is one of the most valuable cost free and pretty much effort free way of doing things you have in your arsenal, but it works extremely well. Keep that in mind all the time, not just throughout this section.

Come back here once you have got your product up and running if you're not working on that right now, because all of these are elements of a sales letter in some way or another, bar two. So lets get started. How about taking it from the top and starting with the most used and widely known and working down to the least widely used, and the new and innovative ideas.

## 5.3. There Are Limits!

Cut off dates and limited numbers: A great place to start and really easy to slip into any sales letter for any product. The old cut off dates are probably the most widely used out of all of these methods, and they seem to still be working.

All this requires is notification of your low price only being guaranteed until a particular date. These are great words to use, because if you do decide to extend the deadline, you'll find that you can without causing a stir.

Way too often recently I've visited sites that say the price will be going up for sure on a particular date, but it never does, and the date magically moves forward each day. Not a good way to be doing business I can assure you. The buying public are getting wise to these obviously false"scarcity tactics" and are singularly unimpressed by them. Done correctly, though, as outlined above, and it works well and doesn't turn your buyers off.

This method is catering more to the impulse buyers rather than adding value, but I thought we'd get that in there too anyway, as it's worth a mention for sure.

## 5.4. Getting It Right

Next up is the limited numbers method: Only allowing a limited number of people into the site at a particular time, or only allowing a particular amount of people to buy at a particular price. Again, quite widely used, and both catering to impulse buyers as well as adding value, depending on which method you're using.

Now this one I especially like. One of my previous sites has this very system up and running, where I only let a few hundred members in at a time. It's a membership site of course, so re-occurring incomes all around for me, and it makes my members feel a little lucky. Some of them have even told me this themselves, and I've had requests from my list on several occasions asking when a spot will become available because they really wanted to get in.

Now you might say that I'm losing money on such a deal, only letting people in a small number at a time, but it really doesn't happen like that. The reason the limit was set in the first place was so that I'd have time to start working on other projects and could run my other sites on autopilot, so you could say I discovered this one by accident.

Don't forget that you can always raise and lower your limits if you do try this, which I highly recommend you do try, even if limiting numbers doesn't suit your situation, limiting numbers on a lower price, very likely will suit every situation, not to mention it always amazes me how far word of mouth travels about this.

## 5.5. Boring Ordinary Testimonials

Next up is the hugely widespread and popular standard testimonial. I'm only going to touch on this, because there really isn't a huge amount to say, and I highly doubt anyone out there has never seen one. A standard section of text either throughout your sales letter, down the side of your nav bar, on a separate page or a database of happy customers works without a problem and goes a long way to cementing in your customers minds that your product and customer service is good. This is especially true if the person or people writing are well known and respected in your field. Try to get in contact with at least one well-known person in your product's marketplace, hand them your product for free, and request a testimonial for it.

## 5.6. A Little Better

Now, let's look at the slightly rarer audio testimonials. These cement value in your product even further and increase customer confidence no end. I've personally seen some text testimonials before, and seen some major flaws that proved without a doubt that they were faked. This pretty much put a big dent in what I thought of these things early on, and I've even had people come to me and tell me they faked their testimonials in the past. Needless to say I wasn't happy about that.

You should never fake a testimonial. That last sentence is so important I want you to go back and read it again. Even if everyone else in your market segment is doing it that's still no excuse. Simply do not do it.

Granted, audio testimonials can be faked too, but it's generally not something that pops into your head when listening compared to reading written ones, hence the big confidence booster and value adding of this method.

If you can get some audio testimonials, whether you ask people to call your answering machine and have them leave messages, or if you're able to record over the net through voice communications, it's well worth it. The extra effort comes in and hits your customers with a massive boost to confidence resulting ultimately in more sales and resources for you and your business. Can't be bad.

One cautionary note about audio testimonials on web sites, do not set them to auto play. That means when a visitor arrives at your site the audio starts. It is annoying and usually off-putting. If people want to hear testimonials, and serious prospects will, they will click a play button.

## 5.7. Testimonials 2.0

Ok, seeing as we've done the audio and text thing with these testimonials, lets go all out, major bells and whistles professionalism with video testimonials. How often do you see streaming video testimonials up on websites? Not very often I'd say. In fact at the time of writing this, I've only seen a handful in the last year, and they were great. Real people giving real accounts of using real products that worked. If any type of testimonial is going to add value to your products, it's going to be this one. A simple idea developed into an all singing all dancing, hard hitting method that works.

Again, a video testimonial can be faked, an actor paid,

but they carry even more weight than an audio testimonial. It could be because people feel that some one wouldn't put their face to a complete fabrication. Some people would, of course, but most people wouldn't want their face attached to a lie. Also another factor is that most people like human contact. Some one talking to you "face to face" as it were is more powerful than hearing a disembodied voice.

The next best thing to the testimonial giver videoing them selves and sending it to you would be inviting these people over to your house to tell you how good the products are. I admit, this is taking things to an extreme, but with all the digital cameras floating around nowadays, and the ability to capture video through the net, and the larger hosting spaces starting to appear through the tough competition, it shouldn't be more than a little time consuming to get a few of these. Well worth it in my opinion. Taking testimonials to the max!

## 5.8. Boring Ordinary Bonuses

Right, I think we've done about as much as we can with those testimonials, so moving on a little to bonuses. Standard bonuses. Nothing fancy really, all you're doing is offering up some sort of additional whatever with the purchase of the product, again adding value. Generally these are known as something directly related to your product, or even better, something that will benefit you as well as the customer getting it for free.

How about putting together a small product training series building your reputation, as well as adding value on the initial sale? It may also reduce your product support costs. Or if you're really on a brainy one that day, how about putting something together that will make you money through educating the buyer? For example, give away an affiliate marketing course to your customers, helping them become better affiliates, allowing them to promote your stuff and make you money at the same time.

## 5.9 More Rewarding Bonuses

It's links like this that make up really clever bonuses, where on the surface they might just seem standard to other people that don't understand where you're coming from. Always try to put something together that will benefit you as well as the customer, whether it's increased sales, a re-branded book packed with affiliate links or links to your product they can give away, or an educational tool that will assist your customer, and put money in your pocket at the same time.

In fact, while we're talking about giving away bonuses to enhance your product, I've even seen some really effective products that are just made up of a bunch of bonuses, with no real central product. Of course they have a central theme, and are all related in some way, but this is something to keep in mind for when you've been going a while and having a slow day. As long as all the products complement each other, and are relevant, they can come together to make a whole new product and income stream for yourself.

## 5.10. Bonuses 2.0

While we're on this subject, please, please take note here, because if I see anyone trying to flog their product, thinking that an e-book entitled ' Doing business today, in the 60's' is going to shift more of their products, I really might have to start wondering about peoples motives. Things like this won't add $500 to your price. In fact, let me tell you how serious this issue is. If you put a dodgy bonus together, or do this in the wrong way, you can devalue your product so much, that it becomes worthless, and you just won't sell any. Simple as that.

So here's a general rule for you. If you've really thought about it, dug around and tried to find something to add in as a good worthwhile bonus to try and tip customers over the sales edge and to have more of them buy your product, and you honestly can't find anything that fits the bill, go with nothing or create an original info product yourself. Having no bonuses are all is better than having one that puts all your customers off. As obvious as that sounds, it seems to be occurring more and more, which is strange, because of the sheer number of people that claim to know what they're talking about that are teaching people what to do with online business nowadays.

Using the example above I want to demonstrate something to you now that also seems to have become a strange epidemic that pretty much makes me and everyone else I know click right off the website and go somewhere else when looking for their products. That is when people take too much time and put in a little too much effort into adding value to one of their products. Or so they think anyway. Have a look at this one, how many times have you seen this recently?

Example: Get your hard hitting, intensive training course,

entitled 'Improve Your Fishing', consisting of two CD's packed with audio and video, showing you all the tricks, tips and tactics in use today by some of the most successful fisherman in the world!. Order now and get this proven course worth over $2500 for a measly $300. In fact, I'm so confident that it's going to help you I'm going to knock the price down further. You can get all this expertise in one place for an amazing $49.95. Order your copy now!

See where I'm coming from? Don't get me wrong, there's nothing wrong with giving special offers to people who buy there and then catering to impulse buyers, and bargain hunters, or just to show people they're getting a really good deal from you, but from $2500 down to $49.95? That's going over the top, and unfortunately just makes your product look like a scam.

For starters, would the course really be worth $2500 full price? It'd have to be pretty spectacular to command that price tag (and could a fishing course ever be worth that much?) and therefore if it was that spectacular why on Earth would you be discounting it that heavily. It just doesn't stack up. It stops looking like phenomenal value and starts screaming scam.

How would you feel if you walked into a store and saw a top of the range 62" plasma screen knocked down from $12000 to $200? I can tell you, your first reaction would either be 'Yeah right, this a joke', or even more likely 'What's the catch?' or 'What's wrong with it?'.

Remember when we talked earlier about increasing customer confidence in your products, and the whole idea of a sales letter is to squish all these problems and questions people might have with a product, while at the same time creating a want, and sometimes even a need for it. Do you see how adding too much value, too soon, or going really over the top with special offer pricing can be detrimental?

Where as you may see it as giving the customers a bargain, they're seeing it as another question in their mind. Another barrier to making that purchase that they need to overcome, or a question they need to find the answer to before they buy your product. It's everywhere nowadays. Discounts aren't bad on their own, but in this type of circumstance, they are going to kill your sales. Most people don't even know why. If you didn't before, now you do. Don't make the same mistake.

Now one thing I don't want to do is let you think that there is only one bad way to add value (or completely remove value) from your products, because I've seen it done over and over again in different circumstances. I was going to give you three examples here, but lets take the fishing example above as number one, and I'm going to give you two more, in totally different situations that will spoil your sales figures. Bear in mind these are real, live examples that are out there right now on the net.

Example two: The 'Only want your bonuses' factor: I land on this pretty blue and white, professionally designed, well built website that immediately makes me smile (Just feels nice when something is presented like this). I proceed to read the sales copy which briefly tells me how I can get money-making tips for free if I sign up to their newsletter. I see links to back issues here too so I'm not really put off by the thoughts of this being another poor excuse to send me ads. Then comes the standard, sign up today and get this freebie. I'm happy, because it looks relevant to what I want to achieve. Now normally at this point I'd just go and sign up, but this person decided to go the extra way to please me.

E-book 1, E-book 2, E-book 3, E-book 4, Software 1, Software 2, Software 3, Software 4,5,6,7 and so on. Now on the surface this might seem like adding value to the point of people not being able to refuse, but honestly, are people signing up to their free newsletter for the freebies or for the content? Again, at first glance getting more subscribers is good right? Well, not really. Not if none of them care about your content and just wanted your collection of fifty thousand e-books. Remember those tire kickers from the previous chapter?. It's really all about quality, not quantity, and this example shows exactly how you can add too much value to a free a product to your detriment. Your quality suffers, so does your pocket, and you've totally wasted your time and effort.

Example three: The 'Not sure what's going on' factor: Here's a good one that I see a lot of, and something else that's on the rise too. In fact, to be honest, I really think this one is our fault, it's us selling these guides that tell you to sell your bonuses like they're products themselves. This is correct information, but it can be taken too far.

Again, I'm surfing around the net and land on a site that happens to be a money making opportunity. I'm not opposed to money making opportunities of course, and this one just happens to have a great headline that entices me to read further. The further I get down the sales letter the better it gets, until we hit the bonuses. E-book one, click here to read about this e-book (forwards me to a whole new sales letter), click here to read about this software (takes me to a whole new sales letter) and so on for three or four bonuses. By the time I'm done, I've been taken all over the place, have five windows open, read six sales letters which each try to sell me on to something else, and have trouble finding my way back to the initial sales letter for the product I wanted to buy in the first place.

It's important to remember to add value using bonuses in a way which makes your bonuses seem like real products themselves, but never ever lose sight of what you want your website to do. Don't throw people off in different directions and have them read ten sales letters for different products. It just doesn't work like that. Again while you may think you're adding value, all you're doing is distracting and confusing your visitors. When people say sell your bonuses like a real product, they mean a few hard hitting paragraphs about how this compliments the main product and you're getting a heck of a good deal, or you can't get it anywhere else, or where it's been proven etc. Don't go over the top, or again, you'll be losing customers.

The three examples above I see every single day, and the worst thing about it is, when people say to me, 'Why am I getting no sales from my site?' and I tell them that parts of their bonuses sections are destroying their sales letter, I get strange looks and comments. See it's like one of those little annoying mind puzzles, where the solution is so obvious people miss it, and I can tell they don't feel too proud about that, but no worries. Not a problem at all, as long as you learn from it and don't repeat the mistake you'll do fine I tell them.

Now if you've read this far and are ultimately confused or lost as to what the heck you could possibly give as a bonus in addition to your product, or don't have anything to hand, don't worry. It doesn't have to be tangible at all. It doesn't have to be an old e-book (in fact, it'd probably be beneficial if it wasn't an old e-book) it doesn't have to be a piece of software. Open your mind a little and think about other things you could offer to people along with your product. Are you respected in your field of expertise? How about a free one hour, no strings phone or video consultation with your customer's purchase, or even a follow-up consultation to see how they've done with the product you've just sold them?

This isn't such a hard thing to implement if you have the knowledge. Personally, I like my free time, and you won't get me talking to you on the phone about your business unless you've just deposited $500 into my account for the hour, and heck, you'd have to know me pretty well and be in my good books to get me down to that price too. Immediately that adds value to this product without me even offering the consultations, because I can tell you now, it took a little longer than three hours to write this guide. This is something you can do too, and if you really wanted there's nothing wrong with going a step further and actually offering those consultations, maybe 30 minutes or an hour per customer free (depending of course on how many customers you plan to get per week. Be careful not to try to give 100 people a free three hour consultation every week).

You don't have to be in the business of selling guides and info about business to put any of this together. It doesn't matter what you're selling, you can use this method somewhere, whether it's an hour free technical support, or a free 30 minute confidence builder to compliment your main product.

It's totally up to you. Be imaginative, and hey, it might even lead to further, paid for, consultations putting even more cash in your pocket. Again, a good freebie helps you, not just your customers. An important factor and a question you should be asking yourself when creating any value adding material. "How does this help me as well as my customers?"

## 5.11. Do You Do Extras?

Before we move on, there's two more ways I'd like to talk to you about adding value to a product. This time, though, the bonuses we'll be offering aren't directly related to the product, and aren't necessarily given on the sales letter as most bonuses are. It's always nice to give the customer a little something extra, and this is one way to do that and again, as we talked about before, helping yourself as well as the customer.

The first example I want to talk about is adding an option for discounts related to your other products, either now, or in the future through a ticket system. A good way to do this is allow customers to add additional products to their shopping cart at a discounted price when they check out. Not only does it allow them something extra for a little less, but it allows you to make more sales at the same time, again, benefiting both you and your customer.

It has also been shown through studies that once you've overcome all of a prospect's objections and they've paid you for one product they're quite likely to be happy paying for more products. This is where up sells and cross sells come in.

If this is the first product you're creating, it doesn't hurt to reward loyalty. How about giving them 10% off the next product they buy from your business? This might not seem like it'll do much on the surface, but when you turn a first time customer into a long term customer that keeps buying from you again and again, this is adding value to your products at it's finest. Because it benefits you the most not just today, but far into the future, where your previous customers are picking up two, three, four, and even more of your products within a year.

This is called "customer life time value". It is what, on average, each customer is worth to your business over the total time that they are a customer of yours. Customers who buy one item and then remove themselves from your list have a value of that initial sale to you. Those that keep on buying and buying from you have a much larger value to you. The average value of a customer will, obviously be somewhere between the two. Once you've been in business for a while you'll be able to work this number out which is vitally important when working out how much to spend on an advertising campaign. No point in spending more than the combined customer value for the number of new customers you expect to generate from it.

Lastly, something that's rather unknown and hardly ever implemented (at least through the products I've purchased over the years anyway) is again, about rewarding loyalty. If for some reason you don't want to include particular bonuses on the sales letter, why not go for something a little different instead, and hit them with it after they buy the product. Granted, you're losing your additional sales power through presenting this on your sales letter, instead handing it out after the sale, but let me assure you, if you do this, you will be remembered. Most importantly people will talk about you (never underestimate the power of word of mouth advertising), and at the same time become long term, loyal customers of yours. Is there anything more valuable?

Above all, if you take nothing else away from this, I want you to remember one thing, and that's that nothing in business is set in stone. No rules that exist now will exist forever, nothing that works now will work forever. The same applies to everything previously written.

Experiment, innovate, be different and you will be remembered, make wads of cash and get your name around, and who knows, in six months time you might just be sitting where I am now, typing out a book manuscript revealing the newest and most cutting edge marketing methods that you've that you've discovered throughout your journey.

## 5.12. Summary

In this section we talked about the concept of adding further value to products and services. We looked at directly influencing your sales through the addition of value, ranging from specifically crafted offers, JV deals, consultations, bonuses and others to demonstrate perceived value.

There are many ways to add value to your product, and the means and methods are forever changing through new and innovative twists on current techniques. It's worth looking out for these the next time you read a powerful sales letter from a trusted marketer, and asking yourself, how are they adding value to their products? Watching how others do things on their sites is one of the most valuable cost free and pretty much effort free way of research that you have in your arsenal, but it works extremely well. Keep that in mind all the time.

A couple of good places to start are cut off dates and limited numbers. Probably the most used and widely known aside from testimonials, these can really get the sales flowing if done correctly.

All the cut off dates require is notification that a special offer is ending on a particular day, giving the impression that the reader will miss out if they don't buy now, an age-old and well-used, but effective, means of pushing home additional sales.

If using this method, use the language that shows that

your low price and your special offer is only guaranteed until a particular date, this way if you decide to continue to a later date it doesn't cause a stir. You should consider actually stopping at the date you specified even though you have left it open (through the language you use) for extension. Only extend if you feel it will greatly benefit your business as people will start lumping you in with all the other fraudulent marketers out there that have never ending sales. You should also avoid using those little java code counters that push the date forwards each day relating to the computer clock time at the visitors end.

Second, think about limited numbers, only allowing a limited number of people into your site a particular point in time. Again, quite widely used, and both catering to impulse buys and adding value. Again, actually limit the number of people, don't say there's only 4 left for ever, that's another sure way to upset your customers and destroy your credibility. You can open again in the future as long as you word your sales page correctly, just make sure you close the offer after the number you say you will and keep it closed for a period of time.

You will likely find you have people emailing you for a spot. You will be building up a list of hungry buyers from this, it would probably be worthwhile sending them a pre-re-opening email offering them the opportunity to take the first spots of the new round of entries to your membership. You are likely to get a very high take up rate.

Testimonials, it will be worth your while taking testimonials to the next level, using audio instead of text or level up again and use video testimonials. These really help with credibility and can help your sales hugely. With cheap webcams and most digital stills cameras capable of recording video it's very easy to record these. Most cell phones have video recording capabilities now a days and the quality will probably be sufficient.

After testimonials we looked at bonuses. Putting together a small training series can be helpful to both you and your customer. Some marketers allow customers to give these courses away as well. This mostly happens when there is an affiliate element to the business. If you can make the training "brandable" by the affiliate they can put their links into it so they gain a commission for product sold off the back of the training. They're happy as they've made a commission and you're happy as you've made another sale that you wouldn't have otherwise. Even if you're not doing an affiliate scheme you still benefit from putting together training as it will likely reduce your tech support load.

Another type of bonus is the related but not additional to the main product bonus. An affiliate marketing guide will help your customer sell your product, it's related, but it's not directly additional to the core product.

Don't add value to the point of taking it away. Old or completely irrelevant bonuses may initially seem to be adding value but the vast majority of your customers will see right through it and put them off. They make you look like you're trying to fob them off with sub-par trash in a desperate attempt to add value to your product. It will do nothing but devalue your product. If you really, truly, can't find a suitable bonus then leave them out, having no bonus is better than having one that will put people off.

Stupid pricing. Initially claiming that your product is worth $x but then crossing it out and saying you'll sell it to them for $y and $y is many, many times lower than $x. That type of ploy makes you look untrustworthy and desperate. It starts ringing alarm bells in the prospect's head and will usually prevent them from becoming a customer.

Another way of effectively perpetrating the same "crime" of stupid pricing is adding a ridiculous quantity of bonuses. If you add too many (some marketers will sell a $100 product that they initially claim is worth $2500 but of course crossed it out and offered it to you for the special $100 price (sound familiar?) and add a claimed $15000 worth of bonuses to it – I've seen it done more than once) bonuses it can devalue the product in the prospect's mind "if the product was good enough they wouldn't need to add all this stuff just to make me buy it" and makes you look desperate "please buy this, look at all this other stuff I'm giving you!".

There are lesser used methods of adding value, a little more subtle and ultimately could be more profitable for you. Try offering discounts for other products at the checkout. "Add this to your cart, and buy them together and save 50%", an excellent and fast way of making double sales in many situations. More cash for you, more value for the customer. Of course not everyone will take up your offer, but the few extra sales sure add up.

You could reward loyalty by giving customers a 10% off coupon code for their next purchase from you. This method is especially good if this is your first product since you won't be able to offer bundle deals as discussed above. But don't think if you're well established with loads of products that you can't use this method as well. There's a company I've bought dozens of products from over the years and now and then then send me a voucher. It increases customer loyalty and creates word of mouth advertising for you due to happy customers.

Last, something that's rather underestimated and hardly ever used The unannounced bonus.

Send them a bonus after they've purchased that you didn't mention in the sales letter.

This method won't help with generating initial sales but it gives your customers a warm and fuzzy feeling and are much more likely to buy from you again in the future and a lot more likely to tell other people how happy with you they are.

The main take away from this chapter as to be "test it!". Nothing in business is set in stone, test everything you can. You won't know how well something works for your business until you test it. You may think you know what will and will not work but when you test you will know. Very often people think they know that something won't work for their business but when it's been tested the find that not only did it work it worked better than the thing they were doing before. Obviously that doesn't happen every time but you'd be surprised how often preconceptions are smashed by testing.

www.ingramcontent.com/pod-product-compliance
Lightning Source LLC
Chambersburg PA
CBHW071648170526
45166CB00003B/1477